DAILY
GRATITUDE
Journal

Simple 52 Week Guide for Expressing Gratitude

This Journal Belongs to:

....

Free Gifts For You!

Visit the Site Below to Download 3 Free E-Books!

https://holistichealershop.com/free/

Introduction

Develop an attitude of gratitude, and give thanks for everything that happens to you, knowing that every step forward is a step toward achieving something bigger and better than your current situation.
Brian Tracy

Learning to be grateful when things go wrong, when problems arise, and when difficulties happen will make a huge difference in your life and the way you will feel about life itself. Life is always better once you feel blessed no matter how difficult things might seem.

Gratitude is seeing life as a beautiful and wonderful gift. Once you feel at peace with the world and about your life, you will find real happiness and contentment.

When everything goes wrong, it is difficult to be in the state of gratitude, but if you remain thankful about even those little blessings you have, your life will become happier and more fulfilling. Learning to be grateful in this ungrateful world is something worth doing.

Give thanks each day and you will see how being grateful for everything you have today can create enormous changes in your life! Thank you and I wish you much love and happiness!

To be yourself in a world that is constantly trying to make you something else is the greatest accomplishment.
Ralph Waldo Emerson

TODAY I AM GRATEFUL FOR: DATE:

1.

2.

3.

Daily Affirmation: The more I accept and love myself, the more I can accept and love others.

TODAY I AM GRATEFUL FOR: DATE:

1.

2.

3.

Daily Affirmation: I have great potential and I'm going to use it.

Go confidently in the direction of your dreams.
Live the life you have imagined.
Henry David Thoreau

TODAY I AM GRATEFUL FOR: DATE:

1.

2.

3.

Daily Affirmation: Every day life gets better & better.

TODAY I AM GRATEFUL FOR: DATE:

1.

2.

3.

Daily Affirmation: I don't have to be perfect; I just choose to be
perfectly me.

Whatever you can do, or dream you can do, begin it.
Boldness has genius, power and magic in it.
Johann Wolfgang von Goethe

TODAY I AM GRATEFUL FOR: DATE: ....

1. ....

2. ....

3. ....

....

Daily Affirmation: *I now recognize my talents and skills.*

TODAY I AM GRATEFUL FOR: DATE: ....

1. ....

2. ....

3. ....

....

Daily Affirmation: *I'm happy being me.*

The more difficulties one has to encounter, within and without, the more significant and the higher in inspiration his life will be.
Horace Bushnell

TODAY I AM GRATEFUL FOR: DATE: ....

1. ....

....

2. ....

....

3. ....

....

Daily Affirmation: *I expect good things to happen.*

THOUGHTS FOR THE WEEK: DATE: ....

....

....

....

....

....

....

....

....

In the confrontation between the stream and the rock, the stream always wins - not through strength, but through persistence.
Buddha

TODAY I AM GRATEFUL FOR: DATE: ....

1. ....
   ....

2. ....
   ....

3. ....
   ....
   ....

Daily Affirmation: *I see something positive in all situations.*

TODAY I AM GRATEFUL FOR: DATE: ....

1. ....
   ....

2. ....
   ....

3. ....
   ....
   ....

Daily Affirmation: *I turn negatives into positives.*

Keep away from those who try to belittle your ambitions. Small people always do that, but the really great make you believe that you too can become great.
Mark Twain

TODAY I AM GRATEFUL FOR: DATE: ....

1. ....

2. ....

3. ....

   ....

Daily Affirmation: *I am sure of my ability to do what is necessary to improve my life.*

TODAY I AM GRATEFUL FOR: DATE: ....

1. ....

2. ....

3. ....

   ....

Daily Affirmation: *If I make mistakes, I am able to give myself the benefit of the doubt.*

When one door of happiness closes, another opens:
but often we look so long at the closed door that
we do not see the one which has been opened for us.
Helen Keller

TODAY I AM GRATEFUL FOR: DATE:

1.

2.

3.

Daily Affirmation: *I am able to take risks and try new things without*
fear.

TODAY I AM GRATEFUL FOR: DATE:

1.

2.

3.

Daily Affirmation: *I am deserving of all the good things in my life.*

Shoot for the moon.
Even if you miss, you'll land among the stars.
Les Brown

TODAY I AM GRATEFUL FOR: DATE: ....

1. ....
....

2. ....
....

3. ....
....

Daily Affirmation: *I am glowing with health and wholeness.*

THOUGHTS FOR THE WEEK: DATE: ....

....
....
....
....
....
....
....
....
....

The greatest discovery of my generation is that a human being can alter his life by altering his attitude.
William James

TODAY I AM GRATEFUL FOR: DATE:

1.

2.

3.

Daily Affirmation: *I behave in ways that promote my health more every day.*

TODAY I AM GRATEFUL FOR: DATE:

1.

2.

3.

Daily Affirmation: *I deserve to be in perfect health.*

There are only two ways to live your life.
One is as though nothing is a miracle.
The other is as though everything is a miracle.
Albert Einstein

TODAY I AM GRATEFUL FOR: DATE: ....

1. ....
....

2. ....
....

3. ....
....

Daily Affirmation: Wealth is pouring into my life.

TODAY I AM GRATEFUL FOR: DATE: ....

1. ....
....

2. ....
....

3. ....
....

Daily Affirmation: I am sailing on the river of wealth.

What we think, we become.
All that we are arises with our thoughts.
With our thoughts, we make the world.
The Buddha

TODAY I AM GRATEFUL FOR: DATE:

1. ....

2. ....

3. ....

....

Daily Affirmation: My body is healthy and functioning
in a very good way.

TODAY I AM GRATEFUL FOR: DATE:

1. ....

2. ....

3. ....

....

Daily Affirmation: I have a lot of energy.

To find what you seek in the road of life,
the best proverb of all is that which says:
"Leave no stone unturned."
Edward Bulwer Lytton

TODAY I AM GRATEFUL FOR: DATE:

1.

2.

3.

Daily Affirmation: My thoughts are under my control.

THOUGHTS FOR THE WEEK: DATE:

If you cry because the sun has gone out of your life, your
tears will prevent you from seeing the stars.
Rabindranath Tagore

TODAY I AM GRATEFUL FOR: DATE:

1.

2.

3.

Daily Affirmation: My mind is calm.

TODAY I AM GRATEFUL FOR: DATE:

1.

2.

3.

Daily Affirmation: I am calm and relaxed in every situation..

Being deeply loved by someone gives you strength, while loving someone deeply gives you courage.
Lao Tzu

TODAY I AM GRATEFUL FOR: DATE: ....

1. ....
   ....

2. ....
   ....

3. ....
   ....

Daily Affirmation: I radiate love and happiness.

TODAY I AM GRATEFUL FOR: DATE: ....

1. ....
   ....

2. ....
   ....

3. ....
   ....

Daily Affirmation: I am surrounded by love.

Happy are those who dream dreams and are ready to pay the price to make them come true.
Leon J. Suenes

TODAY I AM GRATEFUL FOR: DATE:

1.

2.

3.

Daily Affirmation: I have the perfect job for me.

TODAY I AM GRATEFUL FOR: DATE:

1.

2.

3.

Daily Affirmation: I am living in the house of my dreams.

The power of imagination makes us infinite.
John Muir

TODAY I AM GRATEFUL FOR: DATE: ....

1. ....

2. ....

3. ....

....

Daily Affirmation: *I am successful in whatever I do.*

THOUGHTS FOR THE WEEK: DATE: ....

First say to yourself what you would be;
and then do what you have to do.
Epictetus

TODAY I AM GRATEFUL FOR: DATE: ....

1. ....

....

2. ....

....

3. ....

....

Daily Affirmation: *Everything is getting better every day.*

TODAY I AM GRATEFUL FOR: DATE: ....

1. ....

....

2. ....

....

3. ....

....

Daily Affirmation: *I can choose my thoughts at any time.*

Happiness is when what you think, what you say, and
what you do are in harmony.
Anonymous

TODAY I AM GRATEFUL FOR: DATE: ....

1. ....
   ....

2. ....
   ....

3. ....
   ....

Daily Affirmation: I enjoy releasing my limiting beliefs.

TODAY I AM GRATEFUL FOR: DATE: ....

1. ....
   ....

2. ....
   ....

3. ....
   ....

Daily Affirmation: I feel full of energy to accomplish my dreams.

At the touch of love everyone becomes a poet.
Plato

TODAY I AM GRATEFUL FOR: DATE:

1.

2.

3.

Daily Affirmation: *I can meet successfully all the challenges*
I encounter.

TODAY I AM GRATEFUL FOR: DATE:

1.

2.

3.

Daily Affirmation: *My body is perfect the way it is.*

Experience is the child of thought, and thought is the child of action.
Benjamin Disraeli

TODAY I AM GRATEFUL FOR: DATE: ....

1. ....
   ....
2. ....
   ....
3. ....
   ....
   ....

Daily Affirmation: I am always loved.

THOUGHTS FOR THE WEEK: DATE: ....

....
....
....
....
....
....
....
....

*Happy are those who dream dreams and are ready to pay
the price to make them come true.
Leon J. Suenes*

TODAY I AM GRATEFUL FOR: DATE:

1.

2.

3.

Daily Affirmation: I enjoy living my life.

TODAY I AM GRATEFUL FOR: DATE:

1.

2.

3.

Daily Affirmation: I create my own reality.

The power of imagination makes us infinite.
John Muir

TODAY I AM GRATEFUL FOR: DATE: ....

1. ....
....

2. ....
....

3. ....
....

Daily Affirmation: *I always have access to*
internal peace.

TODAY I AM GRATEFUL FOR: DATE: ....

1. ....
....

2. ....
....

3. ....
....

Daily Affirmation: I have all the resources I need at any
given time.

First say to yourself what you would be;
and then do what you have to do.
Epictetus

TODAY I AM GRATEFUL FOR: DATE:

1.

2.

3.

Daily Affirmation: I am supported by loving people.

TODAY I AM GRATEFUL FOR: DATE:

1.

2.

3.

Daily Affirmation: I radiate compassion.

The ability to convert ideas to things is the secret to outward success.
Henry Ward Beecher

TODAY I AM GRATEFUL FOR: DATE: ....

1. ....
   ....

2. ....
   ....

3. ....
   ....

Daily Affirmation: *I treat myself with respect.*

THOUGHTS FOR THE WEEK: DATE: ....

....

....

....

....

....

....

....

Life can be pulled by goals just as surely as it can be pushed by drives.
Viktor Frankl

TODAY I AM GRATEFUL FOR: DATE: ....

1. ....
   ....
2. ....
   ....
3. ....
   ....
   ....

Daily Affirmation: I am open to abundance.

TODAY I AM GRATEFUL FOR: DATE: ....

1. ....
   ....
2. ....
   ....
3. ....
   ....
   ....

Daily Affirmation: I am grateful for the blessings I
receive daily.

There is no happiness except in the realization that we have accomplished something.
Henry Ford

TODAY I AM GRATEFUL FOR: DATE: ....

1. ....
....

2. ....
....

3. ....
....

Daily Affirmation: *I love nutritious healthy food, and I*
enjoy eating fresh
fruits and vegetables.

TODAY I AM GRATEFUL FOR: DATE: ....

1. ....
....

2. ....
....

3. ....
....

Daily Affirmation: I am healthy since my practices are healthy.

The first step in the acquisition of wisdom is silence, the second listening, the third memory, the fourth practice, the fifth teaching others.
Solomon Ibn Gabriol

TODAY I AM GRATEFUL FOR: DATE:

1.

2.

3.

Daily Affirmation: I let go of the past so I can create health now.

TODAY I AM GRATEFUL FOR: DATE:

1.

2.

3.

Daily Affirmation: I am healthy and whole.

A loving heart is the truest wisdom.
Charles Dickens

TODAY I AM GRATEFUL FOR: DATE: ....

1. ....

2. ....

3. ....

....

Daily Affirmation: *I listen to my bodies messages*
with love.

THOUGHTS FOR THE WEEK: DATE: ....

....
....
....
....
....
....
....
....

*One who understands much displays a greater simplicity
of character than one who understands little.*
Alexander Chase

TODAY I AM GRATEFUL FOR: DATE:

1.

2.

3.

Daily Affirmation: I am perfectly healthy in body, mind and
spirit.

TODAY I AM GRATEFUL FOR: DATE:

1.

2.

3.

Daily Affirmation: I am well, I am whole, and I am
strong and healthy.

The man of wisdom is never of two minds;
the man of benevolence never worries;
the man of courage is never afraid.
Confucius

TODAY I AM GRATEFUL FOR: DATE: ....

1. ....
   ....

2. ....
   ....

3. ....
   ....

Daily Affirmation: I am healthy, and full of energy and vitality.

TODAY I AM GRATEFUL FOR: DATE: ....

1. ....
   ....

2. ....
   ....

3. ....
   ....

Daily Affirmation: I am healthy, happy and radiant.

Happiness does not consist in pastimes and amusements
but in virtuous activities.
Aristotle

TODAY I AM GRATEFUL FOR: DATE:

1.

2.

3.

Daily Affirmation: *I have all the energy I need to accomplish my*
goals and to fulfill my desires.

TODAY I AM GRATEFUL FOR: DATE:

1.

2.

3.

Daily Affirmation: God's love heals me and makes me
whole.

Happiness resides not in possessions and not in gold; the feeling of happiness dwells in the soul.
Democritus

TODAY I AM GRATEFUL FOR: DATE:

1.

2.

3.

Daily Affirmation: *My body is healed, restored and filled with energy.*

THOUGHTS FOR THE WEEK: DATE:

People with many interests live, not only longest, but happiest.
George Matthew Allen

TODAY I AM GRATEFUL FOR: DATE: ....

1. ....
   ....
2. ....
   ....
3. ....
   ....

Daily Affirmation: *I have the power to control my health.*

TODAY I AM GRATEFUL FOR: DATE: ....

1. ....
   ....
2. ....
   ....
3. ....
   ....

Daily Affirmation: *I am in control of my health and wellness.*

In the hopes of reaching the moon men fail to see the
flowers that blossom at their feet.
Albert Schweitzer

TODAY I AM GRATEFUL FOR: DATE: ....

1. ....

2. ....

3. ....

Daily Affirmation: *I am healthy in all aspects of my being.*

TODAY I AM GRATEFUL FOR: DATE: ....

1. ....

2. ....

3. ....

Daily Affirmation: *I am always able to maintain my ideal*
weight.

Happiness is not achieved by the conscious pursuit of happiness; it is generally the by-product of other activities.
Aldous Huxley

TODAY I AM GRATEFUL FOR:　　　DATE:

1.

2.

3.

Daily Affirmation: *I am filled with energy to do all the daily activities in my life.*

TODAY I AM GRATEFUL FOR:　　　DATE:

1.

2.

3.

Daily Affirmation: *My mind is at peace.*

There is only one person who could ever make you happy,
and that person is you.
David Burns, Intimate Connections

TODAY I AM GRATEFUL FOR: DATE: ....

1. ....

   ....

2. ....

   ....

3. ....

   ....

Daily Affirmation: *I love and care for my body and it*
cares for me.

THOUGHTS FOR THE WEEK: DATE: ....

....

....

....

....

....

....

....

....

Happiness consists in activity: such is the constitution of our nature; it is a running stream, and not a stagnant pool.
John M. Good

TODAY I AM GRATEFUL FOR: DATE:

1.

2.

3.

Daily Affirmation: I am perfectly healthy in body, mind and spirit.

TODAY I AM GRATEFUL FOR: DATE:

1.

2.

3.

Daily Affirmation: I am well, I am whole, and I am strong and healthy.

Who is the happiest of men? He who values the merits of others, and in their pleasure takes joy, even as though 'twere his own.
Johann Wolfgang von Goethe

TODAY I AM GRATEFUL FOR: DATE:

1.

2.

3.

Daily Affirmation: *I have complete faith in myself.*

TODAY I AM GRATEFUL FOR: DATE:

1.

2.

3.

Daily Affirmation: All the cells of my body are bathed in the perfection of my divine being.

*Happiness is not a matter of events, it depends upon the
tides of the mind.*
Alice Meynell

TODAY I AM GRATEFUL FOR: DATE:

1.

2.

3.

Daily Affirmation: I am healthy, happy and radiant.

TODAY I AM GRATEFUL FOR: DATE:

1.

2.

3.

Daily Affirmation: I radiate good health.

Fortify yourself with contentment, for this is an impregnable fortress.
Epictetus

TODAY I AM GRATEFUL FOR: DATE: ....

1. ....

   ....

2. ....

   ....

3. ....

   ....

Daily Affirmation: *My body is a safe and pleasurable place*
for me to be.

THOUGHTS FOR THE WEEK: DATE: ....

Happiness depends more on the inward disposition of mind
than on outward circumstances.
Benjamin Franklin

TODAY I AM GRATEFUL FOR: DATE:

1.

2.

3.

Daily Affirmation: My sleep is relaxed and refreshing.

TODAY I AM GRATEFUL FOR: DATE:

1.

2.

3.

Daily Affirmation: I have all the energy I need to
accomplish my goals and to
fulfill my desires.

There is only one way to happiness, and that is to cease worrying things which are beyond the power of our will.
Epictetus

TODAY I AM GRATEFUL FOR: DATE: ....

1. ....

2. ....

3. ....

Daily Affirmation: *God's love heals me and makes me whole.*

TODAY I AM GRATEFUL FOR: DATE: ....

1. ....

2. ....

3. ....

Daily Affirmation: *My body is healed, restored and filled with energy.*

You're happiest while you're making the greatest contribution.
Robert F. Kennedy

TODAY I AM GRATEFUL FOR: DATE: ....

1. ....

....

2. ....

....

3. ....

....

....

Daily Affirmation: I am glowing with health and wholeness.

TODAY I AM GRATEFUL FOR: DATE: ....

1. ....

....

2. ....

....

3. ....

....

....

Daily Affirmation: I behave in ways that promote my health more every day.

Action may not always bring happiness;
but there is no happiness without action.
Benjamin Disraeli

TODAY I AM GRATEFUL FOR: DATE: ....

1. ....
   ....

2. ....
   ....

3. ....
   ....

Daily Affirmation: *I deserve to be in perfect health.*

THOUGHTS FOR THE WEEK: DATE: ....

....
....
....
....
....
....
....
....
....

Great effort from great motives is the best definition of a happy life.
William Ellery Channing

TODAY I AM GRATEFUL FOR: DATE: ....

1. ....

2. ....

3. ....

....

Daily Affirmation: I let go of the past so I can create health now.

TODAY I AM GRATEFUL FOR: DATE: ....

1. ....

2. ....

3. ....

....

Daily Affirmation: I create health by expressing love, understanding and compassion.

There is more to life than increasing its speed.
Mahatma Ghandi

TODAY I AM GRATEFUL FOR: DATE: ....

1. ....
   ....
2. ....
   ....
3. ....
   ....

Daily Affirmation: I am healthy in every way.

TODAY I AM GRATEFUL FOR: DATE: ....

1. ....
   ....
2. ....
   ....
3. ....
   ....

Daily Affirmation: Every cell in my body vibrates with energy and health.

The rays of happiness, like those of light, are colorless when unbroken.
Henry W. Longfellow

TODAY I AM GRATEFUL FOR: DATE: ....

1. ....

....

2. ....

....

3. ....

....

Daily Affirmation: I nourish my mind, body and soul.

TODAY I AM GRATEFUL FOR: DATE: ....

1. ....

....

2. ....

....

3. ....

....

Daily Affirmation: My body heals quickly and easily.

*Happiness grows at our own firesides, and is not to be
picked in strangers' gardens.*
Douglas Jerrold

TODAY I AM GRATEFUL FOR: DATE: ....

1. ....

2. ....

3. ....

Daily Affirmation: I am in control of my health and wellness.

THOUGHTS FOR THE WEEK: DATE: ....

Happiness grows at our own firesides, and is not to be picked in strangers' gardens.
Douglas Jerrold

TODAY I AM GRATEFUL FOR: DATE:

1.

2.

3.

Daily Affirmation: *I have abundant energy, vitality and well-being.*

TODAY I AM GRATEFUL FOR: DATE:

1.

2.

3.

Daily Affirmation: *I am healthy in all aspects of my being.*

Happiness is where we find it, but rarely where we seek it.
J. Petit Senn

TODAY I AM GRATEFUL FOR: DATE:

1.

2.

3.

Daily Affirmation: I am always able to maintain my
                              ideal weight.

TODAY I AM GRATEFUL FOR: DATE:

1.

2.

3.

Daily Affirmation: I am filled with energy to do all the daily
                              activities in my life.

Knowledge of what is possible is the beginning of happiness.
George Santayana

TODAY I AM GRATEFUL FOR: DATE:

1.

2.

3.

Daily Affirmation: *My mind is at peace.*

TODAY I AM GRATEFUL FOR: DATE:

1.

2.

3.

Daily Affirmation: *I love and care for my body and it cares for me.*

Our minds are as different as our faces: we are all traveling to one destination; -happiness; but few are going by the same road.
Charles Caleb Colton

TODAY I AM GRATEFUL FOR: DATE: ....

1. ....

....

2. ....

....

3. ....

....

Daily Affirmation: My body is healthy, energized, and perfect in every way.

THOUGHTS FOR THE WEEK: DATE: ....

The only journey is the journey within.
Rainer Maria Rilke

TODAY I AM GRATEFUL FOR: DATE: ....

1. ....
   ....
2. ....
   ....
3. ....
   ....

Daily Affirmation: I am healthy, whole and complete.

TODAY I AM GRATEFUL FOR: DATE: ....

1. ....
   ....
2. ....
   ....
3. ....
   ....

Daily Affirmation: The vibrant wellness in my body increases every day.

Know thyself means this, that you get acquainted with what you know, and what you can do.
Menander

TODAY I AM GRATEFUL FOR: DATE: ....

1. ....

....

2. ....

....

3. ....

....

Daily Affirmation: I am perfectly healthy in body, mind and spirit.

TODAY I AM GRATEFUL FOR: DATE: ....

1. ....

....

2. ....

....

3. ....

....

Daily Affirmation: I am well, I am whole, and I am strong.

Collect as precious pearls the words of the wise and virtuous.
Abd-el-Kadar

TODAY I AM GRATEFUL FOR: DATE:

1.

2.

3.

Daily Affirmation: I am healthy, and full of energy.

TODAY I AM GRATEFUL FOR: DATE:

1.

2.

3.

Daily Affirmation: My entire body functions perfectly.

If we do not plant knowledge when young, it will give us
no shade when we are old.
Lord Chesterfield

TODAY I AM GRATEFUL FOR: DATE: ....

1. ....

....

2. ....

....

3. ....

....

Daily Affirmation: *I radiate good health.*

THOUGHTS FOR THE WEEK: DATE: ....

....

....

....

....

....

....

....

Follow your honest convictions, and stay strong.
William Thackeray

TODAY I AM GRATEFUL FOR: DATE:

1.

2.

3.

Daily Affirmation: I sleep soundly and peacefully.

TODAY I AM GRATEFUL FOR: DATE:

1.

2.

3.

Daily Affirmation: I am living a long and healthy life.

He that will not reflect is a ruined man.
Asian Proverb

TODAY I AM GRATEFUL FOR: DATE: ....

1. ....

   ....

2. ....

   ....

3. ....

   ....

Daily Affirmation: *I have a healthy heart and a*
                       strong set of lungs.

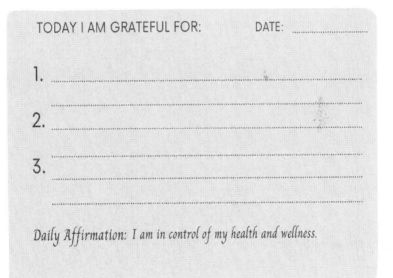

TODAY I AM GRATEFUL FOR: DATE: ....

1. ....

   ....

2. ....

   ....

3. ....

   ....

Daily Affirmation: I am in control of my health and wellness.

Every day do something that will inch you closer to a better tomorrow.
Doug Firebaugh

TODAY I AM GRATEFUL FOR: DATE:

1.

2.

3.

Daily Affirmation: Healthy living ideas flow to me easily.

TODAY I AM GRATEFUL FOR: DATE:

1.

2.

3.

Daily Affirmation: I am living a long and healthy life.

Insist on yourself. Never imitate.
Ralph Waldo Emerson

TODAY I AM GRATEFUL FOR: DATE:

1.

2.

3.

Daily Affirmation: *I eat healthy, nutritious and*
                       digestible food every day.

THOUGHTS FOR THE WEEK: DATE:

Heaven never helps the man who will not act.
Sophocles

TODAY I AM GRATEFUL FOR: DATE:

1.

2.

3.

Daily Affirmation: *I drink large amounts of thirst quenching*
water every day.

TODAY I AM GRATEFUL FOR: DATE:

1.

2.

3.

Daily Affirmation: I have a healthy spirit, mind and body.

Knowing yourself is the beginning of all wisdom.
Aristotle

TODAY I AM GRATEFUL FOR: DATE:

1.

2.

3.

Daily Affirmation: *I have a healing light within me.*

TODAY I AM GRATEFUL FOR: DATE:

1.

2.

3.

Daily Affirmation: *I trust the flow and process of life.*

*In learning to know other things, and other minds, we
become more intimately acquainted with ourselves, and are
to ourselves better worth knowing.*
Philip Gilbert Hamilton

TODAY I AM GRATEFUL FOR: DATE:

1.

2.

3.

Daily Affirmation: I am safe and secure.

TODAY I AM GRATEFUL FOR: DATE:

1.

2.

3.

Daily Affirmation: I am calm and peaceful.

What progress, you ask, have I made? I have begun to be
a friend to myself.
Hecato, Greek philosopher

TODAY I AM GRATEFUL FOR: DATE: ....

1. ....
....

2. ....
....

3. ....
....

Daily Affirmation: *I am strong and hopeful.*

THOUGHTS FOR THE WEEK: DATE: ....

We are either progressing or retrograding all the while;
there is no such thing as remaining stationary in this life.
James Freeman Clarke

TODAY I AM GRATEFUL FOR: DATE:

1.
2.
3.

Daily Affirmation: I am part of a Universal plan.

TODAY I AM GRATEFUL FOR: DATE:

1.
2.
3.

Daily Affirmation: I love and appreciate myself.

To conquer oneself is the best and noblest victory; to be vanquished by one's own nature is the worst and most ignoble defeat.
Plato

TODAY I AM GRATEFUL FOR: DATE: ....

1. ....
....
2. ....
....
3. ....
....
....

Daily Affirmation: *I am capable and healthy.*

TODAY I AM GRATEFUL FOR: DATE: ....

1. ....
....
2. ....
....
3. ....
....
....

Daily Affirmation: *I am powerful.*

Everybody wants to be somebody; nobody wants to grow.
Johann Wolfgang von Goethe

TODAY I AM GRATEFUL FOR: DATE:

1.

2.

3.

Daily Affirmation: *My surroundings are safe and friendly.*

TODAY I AM GRATEFUL FOR: DATE:

1.

2.

3.

Daily Affirmation: *I am at peace.*

The happiest life is that which constantly exercises and educates what is best in us.
Hamerton

TODAY I AM GRATEFUL FOR: DATE: ....

1. ....
   ....
2. ....
   ....
3. ....
   ....

Daily Affirmation: I send others my love.

THOUGHTS FOR THE WEEK: DATE: ....

....
....
....
....
....
....
....
....
....

We only become what we are by the radical and deep-seated refusal of that which others have made of us.
Jean-Paul Sartre

TODAY I AM GRATEFUL FOR: DATE:

1.

2.

3.

Daily Affirmation: I am filled with love.

TODAY I AM GRATEFUL FOR: DATE:

1.

2.

3.

Daily Affirmation: My needs will always be taken care of.

Change and growth take place when a person has risked himself and dares to become involved with experimenting with his own life.
Herbert Otto

TODAY I AM GRATEFUL FOR: DATE:

1. ....

2. ....

3. ....

Daily Affirmation: *I move forward with love and trust.*

TODAY I AM GRATEFUL FOR: DATE:

1. ....

2. ....

3. ....

Daily Affirmation: Life supports and sustains me.

*Heed the still small voice that so seldom leads us wrong, and
never into folly.*
Marquise du Deffand

TODAY I AM GRATEFUL FOR: DATE: ....

1. ....
   ....
2. ....
   ....
3. ....

   ....

Daily Affirmation: I let go and trust.

TODAY I AM GRATEFUL FOR: DATE: ....

1. ....
   ....
2. ....
   ....
3. ....

   ....

Daily Affirmation: I welcome the new in my life.

Your real influence is measured by your treatment of yourself.
A. Bronson Alcott

TODAY I AM GRATEFUL FOR: DATE:

1.

2.

3.

Daily Affirmation: I live in joy and peace.

THOUGHTS FOR THE WEEK: DATE:

Energy and persistence conquer all things.
Benjamin Franklin

TODAY I AM GRATEFUL FOR: DATE: ....

1. ....

....

2. ....

....

3. ....

....

Daily Affirmation: *I now resolve any long standing problems.*

TODAY I AM GRATEFUL FOR: DATE: ....

1. ....

....

2. ....

....

3. ....

....

Daily Affirmation: I care for myself with love and respect.

If we all did the things we are capable of,
we would astound ourselves.
Thomas Edison

TODAY I AM GRATEFUL FOR: DATE: ....

1. ....

....

2. ....

....

3. ....

....

Daily Affirmation: *I am important and worthwhile.*

TODAY I AM GRATEFUL FOR: DATE: ....

1. ....

....

2. ....

....

3. ....

....

Daily Affirmation: I nourish myself and my needs.

A man who finds no satisfaction in himself will seek for it in vain elsewhere.
La Rochefoucauld

TODAY I AM GRATEFUL FOR:　　DATE:

1.

2.

3.

Daily Affirmation:　*I release all anger, sadness, grief and resentment.*

TODAY I AM GRATEFUL FOR:　　DATE:

1.

2.

3.

Daily Affirmation:　*I lovingly forgive everyone, including myself.*

Fear less, hope more, eat less, chew more, whine less,
breathe more, talk less, say more, hate less, love more, and
good things will be yours.
Swedish Proverb

TODAY I AM GRATEFUL FOR: DATE:

1.

2.

3.

Daily Affirmation: *I choose to fill my world with*
joy and peace.

THOUGHTS FOR THE WEEK: DATE:

Exert your talents, and distinguish yourself, and don't think of retiring from the world, until the world will be sorry that you retire.
Samuel Johnson

TODAY I AM GRATEFUL FOR: DATE: ....

1. ....

....

2. ....

....

3. ....

....

Daily Affirmation: I love my life.

TODAY I AM GRATEFUL FOR: DATE: ....

1. ....

....

2. ....

....

3. ....

....

Daily Affirmation: I create love and joy wherever I go.

You must look into other people as well as at them.
Lord Chesterfield

TODAY I AM GRATEFUL FOR: DATE: ....

1. ....
....

2. ....
....

3. ....
....

Daily Affirmation: *I release the old that no longer serves me.*

TODAY I AM GRATEFUL FOR: DATE: ....

1. ....
....

2. ....
....

3. ....
....

Daily Affirmation: *I allow life to flow through me.*

You must look into other people as well as at them.
Lord Chesterfield

TODAY I AM GRATEFUL FOR: DATE:

1.

2.

3.

Daily Affirmation: *I release the old that no longer serves me.*

TODAY I AM GRATEFUL FOR: DATE:

1.

2.

3.

Daily Affirmation: *I allow life to flow through me.*

A good deed is never lost: he who sows courtesy reaps friendship; and he who plants kindness gathers love.
Basil

TODAY I AM GRATEFUL FOR: DATE:

1.

2.

3.

Daily Affirmation: *I share what I have.*

THOUGHTS FOR THE WEEK: DATE:

The secret of many a man's success in the world resides in his insight into the moods of men and his tact in dealing with them.
J. G. Holland

TODAY I AM GRATEFUL FOR: DATE:

1.

2.

3.

Daily Affirmation: I create a life I love.

TODAY I AM GRATEFUL FOR: DATE:

1.

2.

3.

Daily Affirmation: I experience the sweetness of life.

To rejoice in another's prosperity, is to give content to your own lot: to mitigate another's grief, is to alleviate or dispel your own.
Thomas Edwards

TODAY I AM GRATEFUL FOR: DATE: ....

1. ....

....

2. ....

....

3. ....

....

Daily Affirmation: *I fill every moment with joy.*

TODAY I AM GRATEFUL FOR: DATE: ....

1. ....

....

2. ....

....

3. ....

....

Daily Affirmation: *I let go of sorrow and control.*

To rejoice in another's prosperity, is to give content to your own lot: to mitigate another's grief, is to alleviate or dispel your own.
Thomas Edwards

TODAY I AM GRATEFUL FOR: DATE:

1.

2.

3.

Daily Affirmation: *I fill every moment with joy.*

TODAY I AM GRATEFUL FOR: DATE:

1.

2.

3.

Daily Affirmation: *I let go of sorrow and control.*

Charity, good behavior, amiable speech, unselfishness —
these by the chief sage have been declared the elements of
popularity.
Burmese Proverb

TODAY I AM GRATEFUL FOR: DATE: ....

1. ....

2. ....

3. ....

....

Daily Affirmation: I release all fear and rejection.

THOUGHTS FOR THE WEEK: DATE: ....

Be courteous to all, but intimate with few;
and let those be well-tried before you give them your
confidence.
George Washington

TODAY I AM GRATEFUL FOR: DATE:

1.

2.

3.

Daily Affirmation: I love what I do.

TODAY I AM GRATEFUL FOR: DATE:

1.

2.

3.

Daily Affirmation: I am the center of love and joy.

Look to be treated by others as you have treated others.
Publius Syrus

TODAY I AM GRATEFUL FOR: DATE: ....

1. ....
....

2. ....
....

3. ....
....

Daily Affirmation: My heart beats with love and compassion.

TODAY I AM GRATEFUL FOR: DATE: ....

1. ....
....

2. ....
....

3. ....
....

Daily Affirmation: I express my love for others.

Look to be treated by others as you have treated others.
Publius Syrus

TODAY I AM GRATEFUL FOR: DATE: ....

1. ....

2. ....

3. ....

Daily Affirmation: *My heart beats with love and compassion.*

TODAY I AM GRATEFUL FOR: DATE: ....

1. ....

2. ....

3. ....

Daily Affirmation: *I express my love for others.*

Success in life, in anything, depends upon the number of persons that one can make himself agreeable to.
Thomas Carlyle

TODAY I AM GRATEFUL FOR: DATE:

1.

2.

3.

Daily Affirmation: I am no longer afraid.

THOUGHTS FOR THE WEEK: DATE:

Let us believe neither half of the good people tell us of ourselves, nor half of the evil they say of others.
J. Petit Senn

TODAY I AM GRATEFUL FOR: DATE:

1.

2.

3.

Daily Affirmation: I slip into peaceful sleep.

TODAY I AM GRATEFUL FOR: DATE:

1.

2.

3.

Daily Affirmation: I look forward to the rest of my life.

The more you say, the less people remember.
François Fénelon

TODAY I AM GRATEFUL FOR:　　　DATE: ....

1. ....
....
2. ....
....
3. ....
....

Daily Affirmation: I am balanced and peaceful.

TODAY I AM GRATEFUL FOR:　　　DATE: ....

1. ....
....
2. ....
....
3. ....
....

Daily Affirmation: Angels bless me with love.

The more you say, the less people remember.
François Fénelon

TODAY I AM GRATEFUL FOR: DATE:

1.

2.

3.

Daily Affirmation: I am balanced and peaceful.

TODAY I AM GRATEFUL FOR: DATE:

1.

2.

3.

Daily Affirmation: Angels bless me with love.

Never lose a chance of saying a kind word.
William Thackeray

TODAY I AM GRATEFUL FOR: DATE: ....

1. ....
   ....
2. ....
   ....
3. ....
   ....

Daily Affirmation: *I am in charge of me.*

THOUGHTS FOR THE WEEK: DATE: ....

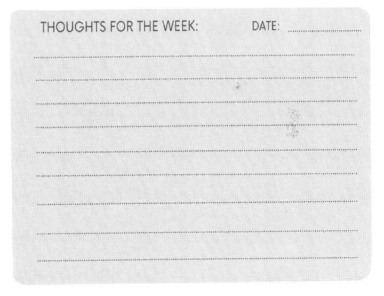

It is always good to know, if only in passing, charming human beings. It refreshes one like flowers and woods and clear brooks.
George Eliot

TODAY I AM GRATEFUL FOR: DATE:

1.

2.

3.

Daily Affirmation: *I am strong and flexible.*

TODAY I AM GRATEFUL FOR: DATE:

1.

2.

3.

Daily Affirmation: *I am strong and powerful.*

Every man is a volume if you know how to read him.
William Ellery Channing

TODAY I AM GRATEFUL FOR: DATE: ....

1. ....
   ....

2. ....
   ....

3. ....
   ....
   ....

Daily Affirmation: *I am protected by angels.*

TODAY I AM GRATEFUL FOR: DATE: ....

1. ....
   ....

2. ....
   ....

3. ....
   ....

Daily Affirmation: I forgive myself and others.

Every man is a volume if you know how to read him.
William Ellery Channing

TODAY I AM GRATEFUL FOR: DATE:

1.

2.

3.

Daily Affirmation: I am protected by angels.

TODAY I AM GRATEFUL FOR: DATE:

1.

2.

3.

Daily Affirmation: I forgive myself and others.

The less people speak of their greatness,
the more we think of it.
Lord Bacon

TODAY I AM GRATEFUL FOR: DATE:

1.

2.

3.

Daily Affirmation: I love the cycles of my life.

THOUGHTS FOR THE WEEK: DATE:

A good word is an easy obligation; but not to speak ill
requires only our silence; which costs us nothing.
John Tillotson

TODAY I AM GRATEFUL FOR: DATE:

1.

2.

3.

Daily Affirmation: *I support my own ideas.*

TODAY I AM GRATEFUL FOR: DATE:

1.

2.

3.

Daily Affirmation: I give myself love and approval.

It requires less character to discover the faults of others
than is does to tolerate them.
J. Petit Senn

TODAY I AM GRATEFUL FOR: DATE:

1.

2.

3.

Daily Affirmation: I am awesome.

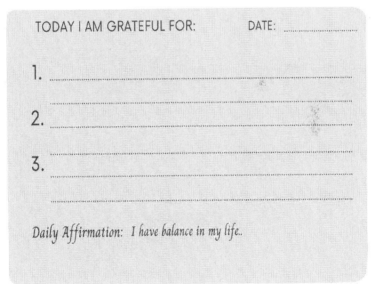

TODAY I AM GRATEFUL FOR: DATE:

1.

2.

3.

Daily Affirmation: I have balance in my life..

*It requires less character to discover the faults of others
than is does to tolerate them.*
J. Petit Senn

TODAY I AM GRATEFUL FOR: DATE:

1.

2.

3.

Daily Affirmation: *I am awesome.*

TODAY I AM GRATEFUL FOR: DATE:

1.

2.

3.

Daily Affirmation: *I have balance in my life..*

Do not forget small kindnesses and do not remember small faults.
Chinese Proverb

TODAY I AM GRATEFUL FOR: DATE: ....

1. ....

2. ....

3. ....

Daily Affirmation: *Every day my mind is filled with positive thoughts.*

THOUGHTS FOR THE WEEK: DATE: ....

It is hard to fail, but it is worse never to have tried to succeed.
Theodore Roosevelt

TODAY I AM GRATEFUL FOR: DATE:

1.

2.

3.

Daily Affirmation: I am healthy.

TODAY I AM GRATEFUL FOR: DATE:

1.

2.

3.

Daily Affirmation: I have vitality.

Half of the failures in life come from pulling one's horse
when he is leaping.
Thomas Hood

TODAY I AM GRATEFUL FOR: DATE: ....

1. ....

2. ....

3. ....

Daily Affirmation: *I am loosing weight as I eat right.*

TODAY I AM GRATEFUL FOR: DATE: ....

1. ....

2. ....

3. ....

Daily Affirmation: *I know that my healing is already*
in process.

Half of the failures in life come from pulling one's horse when he is leaping.
Thomas Hood

TODAY I AM GRATEFUL FOR: DATE:

1.

2.

3.

Daily Affirmation: *I am loosing weight as I eat right.*

TODAY I AM GRATEFUL FOR: DATE:

1.

2.

3.

Daily Affirmation: *I know that my healing is already in process.*

I failed my way to success.
Thomas Edison

TODAY I AM GRATEFUL FOR: DATE: ....

1. ....

   ....

2. ....

   ....

3. ....

   ....

Daily Affirmation: Every cell in my body vibrates with energy and health.

THOUGHTS FOR THE WEEK: DATE: ....

....

....

....

....

....

....

....

....

Every failure brings with it the seed of an equivalent success.
Napoleon Hill

TODAY I AM GRATEFUL FOR: DATE:

1.

2.

3.

Daily Affirmation: *I naturally make choices that are good for me.*

TODAY I AM GRATEFUL FOR: DATE:

1.

2.

3.

Daily Affirmation: *I take loving care of my body and my body*
responds with health, an abundance of energy
and a wonderful feeling of well-being.

Failure is blindness to the strategic element in events;
success is readiness for instant action when the opportune
moment arrives.
Newell D. Hillis

TODAY I AM GRATEFUL FOR: DATE:

1.

2.

3.

Daily Affirmation: My body heals quickly and easily.

TODAY I AM GRATEFUL FOR: DATE:

1.

2.

3.

Daily Affirmation: I am perfectly healthy in body, mind and spirit.

*Failure is blindness to the strategic element in events;
success is readiness for instant action when the opportune
moment arrives.*
Newell D. Hillis

TODAY I AM GRATEFUL FOR: DATE:

1.

2.

3.

Daily Affirmation: *My body heals quickly and easily.*

TODAY I AM GRATEFUL FOR: DATE:

1.

2.

3.

Daily Affirmation: *I am perfectly healthy in body, mind and spirit.*

They fail, and they alone, who have not striven.
Thomas Bailey Aldrich

TODAY I AM GRATEFUL FOR: DATE: ....

1. ....

   ....

2. ....

   ....

3. ....

   ....

Daily Affirmation: *I am well, I am whole, and I am strong*
and healthy..

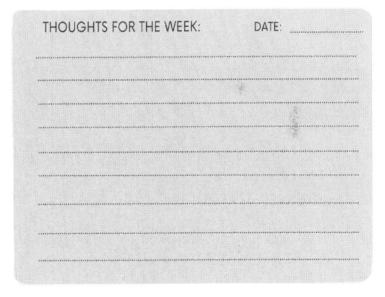

THOUGHTS FOR THE WEEK: DATE: ....

I was never afraid of failure, for I would sooner fail
than not be among the best.
John Keats

TODAY I AM GRATEFUL FOR: DATE:

1.

2.

3.

Daily Affirmation: My body is a safe and pleasurable place
for me to be.

TODAY I AM GRATEFUL FOR: DATE:

1.

2.

3.

Daily Affirmation: My sleep is relaxed and refreshing.

He that is down needs fear no fall.
John Bunyan

TODAY I AM GRATEFUL FOR: DATE:

1. ....
....
2. ....
....
3. ....
....

Daily Affirmation: I have all the energy I need to accomplish
my goals.

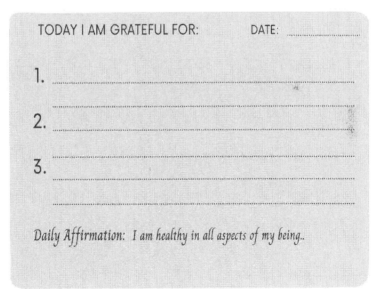

TODAY I AM GRATEFUL FOR: DATE:

1. ....
....
2. ....
....
3. ....
....

Daily Affirmation: I am healthy in all aspects of my being..

He that is down needs fear no fall.
John Bunyan

TODAY I AM GRATEFUL FOR: DATE:

1.

2.

3.

Daily Affirmation: *I have all the energy I need to accomplish*
my goals.

TODAY I AM GRATEFUL FOR: DATE:

1.

2.

3.

Daily Affirmation: *I am healthy in all aspects of my being..*

Never let the fear of striking out get in your way.
George Herman "Babe" Ruth

TODAY I AM GRATEFUL FOR: DATE:

1. ....
   ....
2. ....
   ....
3. ....
   ....

Daily Affirmation: *My thoughts and ideas have power.*

THOUGHTS FOR THE WEEK: DATE:

The greatest mistake you can make in life is to
continually be afraid you will make one.
Elbert Hubbard

TODAY I AM GRATEFUL FOR: DATE:

1.

2.

3.

Daily Affirmation: *I love and care for my body and it*
cares for me.

TODAY I AM GRATEFUL FOR: DATE:

1.

2.

3.

Daily Affirmation: *I love and bless my body as a physical*
manifestation of my soul.

Little minds are tamed and subdued by misfortunes; but great minds rise above them.
Washington Irving

TODAY I AM GRATEFUL FOR: DATE:

1.

2.

3.

Daily Affirmation: *I love and approve of myself and my body.*

TODAY I AM GRATEFUL FOR: DATE:

1.

2.

3.

Daily Affirmation: *My whole body, mind and soul are one and I listen to my body's messages..*

Little minds are tamed and subdued by misfortunes; but great minds rise above them.
Washington Irving

TODAY I AM GRATEFUL FOR: DATE:

1.

2.

3.

Daily Affirmation: I love and approve of myself and my body.

TODAY I AM GRATEFUL FOR: DATE:

1.

2.

3.

Daily Affirmation: My whole body, mind and soul are one and I listen to my body's messages..

Our greatest glory consist not in never falling, but in
rising every time we fall.
Oliver Goldsmith

TODAY I AM GRATEFUL FOR: DATE: ....

1. ....
....

2. ....
....

3. ....
....

Daily Affirmation: *I listen to my body's message with*
gratefulness and love.

THOUGHTS FOR THE WEEK: DATE: ....

....
....
....
....
....
....
....
....
....

What would life be if we had no courage to attempt anything?
Vincent van Gogh

TODAY I AM GRATEFUL FOR: DATE:

1.

2.

3.

Daily Affirmation: *I live a healthy and balanced life.*

TODAY I AM GRATEFUL FOR: DATE:

1.

2.

3.

Daily Affirmation: *I always contribute in healthy ways to my body..*

There is no failure except in no longer trying.
Elbert Hubbard

TODAY I AM GRATEFUL FOR: DATE:

1.

2.

3.

Daily Affirmation: I am in excellent health.

TODAY I AM GRATEFUL FOR: DATE:

1.

2.

3.

Daily Affirmation: All my organs and systems are functioning properly.

There is no failure except in no longer trying.
Elbert Hubbard

TODAY I AM GRATEFUL FOR: DATE: ....

1. ....

....

2. ....

....

3. ....

....

Daily Affirmation: *I am in excellent health.*

TODAY I AM GRATEFUL FOR: DATE: ....

1. ....

....

2. ....

....

3. ....

....

Daily Affirmation: *All my organs and systems are*
functioning properly.

There is no impossibility to him who stands prepared to conquer every hazard. The fearful are the failing.
Sarah J. Hale

TODAY I AM GRATEFUL FOR: DATE: ....

1. ....
   ....
2. ....
   ....
3. ....
   ....

Daily Affirmation: I am healthy, relaxed, and free of pain and disease.

THOUGHTS FOR THE WEEK: DATE: ....

....
....
....
....
....
....
....
....

Failure teaches success.
Japanese Saying

TODAY I AM GRATEFUL FOR: DATE: ....

1. ....

2. ....

3. ....

....

Daily Affirmation: *Every day in every way, I am*
getting better and better.

TODAY I AM GRATEFUL FOR: DATE: ....

1. ....

2. ....

3. ....

....

Daily Affirmation: *I am in the flow of life, and I am grateful*
for the gift of being alive.

Don't waste your life in doubts and fears: spend yourself on the work before you, well assured that the right performance of this hour's duties will be the best preparation for the hours or ages that follow it.
Ralph Waldo Emerson

TODAY I AM GRATEFUL FOR: DATE: ....

1. ....
....

2. ....
....

3. ....
....

Daily Affirmation: My life is my own and I easily resolve my conflicts.

TODAY I AM GRATEFUL FOR: DATE: ....

1. ....
....

2. ....
....

3. ....
....

Daily Affirmation: I am successful in everything I do.

*Don't waste your life in doubts and fears: spend yourself
on the work before you, well assured that the right
performance of this hour's duties will be the best
preparation for the hours or ages that follow it.*
Ralph Waldo Emerson

TODAY I AM GRATEFUL FOR: DATE:

1.

2.

3.

Daily Affirmation: My life is my own and I easily
                                resolve my conflicts.

TODAY I AM GRATEFUL FOR: DATE:

1.

2.

3.

Daily Affirmation: I am successful in everything I do.

No longer forward nor behind I look in hope and fear;
But grateful take the good I find, The best of now and here.
John G. Whittier

TODAY I AM GRATEFUL FOR: DATE:

1.

2.

3.

Daily Affirmation: I am joyfully receiving wealth and
abundance in my life.

THOUGHTS FOR THE WEEK: DATE:

Be just, and fear not.
Let all the ends thou aim'st at be thy country's,
Thy God's and truth's.
William Shakespeare

TODAY I AM GRATEFUL FOR: DATE:

1.

2.

3.

Daily Affirmation: I am a rich person.

TODAY I AM GRATEFUL FOR: DATE:

1.

2.

3.

Daily Affirmation: Money enhances my positive power.

Never let life's hardships disturb you ...no one can avoid problems, not even saints or sages.
Nichiren Daishonen

TODAY I AM GRATEFUL FOR: DATE: ....

1. ....
   ....
2. ....
   ....
3. ....
   ....

Daily Affirmation: I love life.

TODAY I AM GRATEFUL FOR: DATE: ....

1. ....
   ....
2. ....
   ....
3. ....
   ....

Daily Affirmation: I am a loving person.

Never let life's hardships disturb you ...no one can avoid problems, not even saints or sages.
Nichiren Daishonen

TODAY I AM GRATEFUL FOR: DATE: ....

1. ....

2. ....

3. ....

....

Daily Affirmation: *I love life.*

TODAY I AM GRATEFUL FOR: DATE: ....

1. ....

2. ....

3. ....

....

Daily Affirmation: *I am a loving person.*

Ask yourself this question:
"Will this matter a year from now?"
Richard Carlson

TODAY I AM GRATEFUL FOR: DATE:

1.

2.

3.

Daily Affirmation: *I am successful and I love it.*

THOUGHTS FOR THE WEEK: DATE:

Do not anticipate trouble, or worry about what may never happen. Keep in the sunlight.
Benjamin Franklin

TODAY I AM GRATEFUL FOR: DATE:

1.

2.

3.

Daily Affirmation: *I will reach my goals, joyfully and easily.*

TODAY I AM GRATEFUL FOR: DATE:

1.

2.

3.

Daily Affirmation: *I am so happy to be alive.*

Imagine every day to be the last of a life surrounded
with hopes, cares, anger and fear. The hours that come
unexpectedly will be much the more grateful.
Horace

TODAY I AM GRATEFUL FOR: DATE: ....

1. ....

....

2. ....

....

3. ....

....

Daily Affirmation: *Life always holds out as much goodness as I*
am willing to accept.

TODAY I AM GRATEFUL FOR: DATE: ....

1. ....

....

2. ....

....

3. ....

....

Daily Affirmation: *Life rewards me with abundance.*

Imagine every day to be the last of a life surrounded with hopes, cares, anger and fear. The hours that come unexpectedly will be much the more grateful.
Horace

TODAY I AM GRATEFUL FOR: DATE:

1.

2.

3.

Daily Affirmation: *Life always holds out as much goodness as I am willing to accept.*

TODAY I AM GRATEFUL FOR: DATE:

1.

2.

3.

Daily Affirmation: *Life rewards me with abundance.*

The mind that is anxious about future events is
miserable.
Seneca

TODAY I AM GRATEFUL FOR: DATE: ....

1. ....
   ....
2. ....
   ....
3. ....
   ....
   ....

Daily Affirmation: *I deserve to be wealthy, rich, prosperous*
and affluent.

THOUGHTS FOR THE WEEK: DATE: ....

....
....
....
....
....
....
....
....

Let us be of good cheer, remembering that the misfortunes
hardest to bear are those that never happen.
James Russel Lowell

TODAY I AM GRATEFUL FOR: DATE:

1.

2.

3.

Daily Affirmation: *I am now earning a great big income doing*
what satisfies me.

TODAY I AM GRATEFUL FOR: DATE:

1.

2.

3.

Daily Affirmation: *Something wonderful is happening to me*
today-I can feel it!

Live in each season as it passes; breathe the air, drink the drink, taste the fruit, and resign yourself to the influences of each.
Henry David Thoreau

TODAY I AM GRATEFUL FOR: DATE:

1.

2.

3.

Daily Affirmation: *Money comes to me easily and effortlessly, waking and sleeping.*

TODAY I AM GRATEFUL FOR: DATE:

1.

2.

3.

Daily Affirmation: *Abundance surrounds me.*

Live in each season as it passes; breathe the air, drink the drink, taste the fruit, and resign yourself to the influences of each.
Henry David Thoreau

TODAY I AM GRATEFUL FOR: DATE:

1. ....

2. ....

3. ....

....

Daily Affirmation: Money comes to me easily and effortlessly, waking and sleeping.

TODAY I AM GRATEFUL FOR: DATE:

1. ....

2. ....

3. ....

....

Daily Affirmation: Abundance surrounds me.

I never think of the future - it comes soon enough.
Albert Einstein

TODAY I AM GRATEFUL FOR: DATE: ....

1. ....
....

2. ....
....

3. ....
....

Daily Affirmation: *I release all feelings of lack and limitation and*
gratefully accept blessings of joy and abundance.

THOUGHTS FOR THE WEEK: DATE: ....

....
....
....
....
....
....
....
....
....
....

Adventure is worthwhile.
Amelia Earhart

TODAY I AM GRATEFUL FOR:　　　　DATE: ....

1. ....
   ....
2. ....
   ....
3. ....
   ....

Daily Affirmation: *I recognize and embrace my ability to manifest*
my desires.

TODAY I AM GRATEFUL FOR:　　　　DATE: ....

1. ....
   ....
2. ....
   ....
3. ....
   ....

Daily Affirmation: *The universe naturally and freely provides for all*
my needs.

Challenges are what make life interesting; overcoming them is what makes life meaningful.
Joshua J. Marine

TODAY I AM GRATEFUL FOR: DATE: ....

1. ....

....

2. ....

....

3. ....

....

Daily Affirmation: *I expect and welcome good fortune abundantly at every moment of my life.*

TODAY I AM GRATEFUL FOR: DATE: ....

1. ....

....

2. ....

....

3. ....

....

Daily Affirmation: *I have unlimited abundance.*

*Challenges are what make life interesting; overcoming them
is what makes life meaningful.*
Joshua J. Marine

TODAY I AM GRATEFUL FOR: DATE:

1.

2.

3.

Daily Affirmation: I expect and welcome good fortune abundantly
at every moment of my life.

TODAY I AM GRATEFUL FOR: DATE:

1.

2.

3.

Daily Affirmation: I have unlimited abundance.

Difficulties are meant to rouse, not discourage. The human spirit is to grow strong by conflict.
William Ellery Channing

TODAY I AM GRATEFUL FOR: DATE: ....

1. ....
....

2. ....
....

3. ....
....

....

Daily Affirmation: *Learning new things satisfies my soul.*

THOUGHTS FOR THE WEEK: DATE: ....

....

....

....

....

....

....

....

....

It is not good for all our wishes to be filled; through sickness we recognize the value of health; through evil, the value of good; through hunger, the value of food; through exertion, the value of rest.
- Greek Proverb

TODAY I AM GRATEFUL FOR: DATE: ....

1. ....

2. ....

3. ....

....

Daily Affirmation: *I am passionate about building wealth.*

TODAY I AM GRATEFUL FOR: DATE: ....

1. ....

2. ....

3. ....

....

Daily Affirmation: *God provides me with more than enough abundance in my life.*

We are like tea bags - we don't know man lying on sidewalk as people pass by our own strength until we're in hot water.
Sister Busche

TODAY I AM GRATEFUL FOR: DATE:

1.

2.

3.

Daily Affirmation: I am easily accepting abundance in my life now.

TODAY I AM GRATEFUL FOR: DATE:

1.

2.

3.

Daily Affirmation: I am financially secure.

We are like tea bags - we don't know man lying on sidewalk as people pass by our own strength until we're in hot water.
Sister Busche

TODAY I AM GRATEFUL FOR: DATE:

1.

2.

3.

Daily Affirmation: *I am easily accepting abundance in my life now.*

TODAY I AM GRATEFUL FOR: DATE:

1.

2.

3.

Daily Affirmation: *I am financially secure.*

There are two ways of meeting difficulties: you alter the difficulties, or you alter yourself to meet them.
Phyllis Battome

TODAY I AM GRATEFUL FOR: DATE: ....

1. ....
   ....
2. ....
   ....
3. ....
   ....
   ....

Daily Affirmation: *I open myself to receive the abundance
of The Universe.*

THOUGHTS FOR THE WEEK: DATE: ....

....
....
....
....
....
....
....
....
....

A man is but the product of his thoughts what he thinks, he becomes.
Mohandas Gandhi

TODAY I AM GRATEFUL FOR: DATE: ....

1. ....

2. ....

3. ....

....

Daily Affirmation: *Through the power of my subconscious mind, I effortlessly attract all the wealth I need and desire.*

TODAY I AM GRATEFUL FOR: DATE: ....

1. ....

2. ....

3. ....

....

Daily Affirmation: *I will stay focused on my goals until I achieve them.*

If we are to teach real peace in this world, and if we are to carry on a real war against war, we shall have to begin with the children.
Mohandas Gandhi

TODAY I AM GRATEFUL FOR: DATE: ....

1. ....
   ....
2. ....
   ....
3. ....
   ....

Daily Affirmation: I live an independent life that I choose to design however I want.

TODAY I AM GRATEFUL FOR: DATE: ....

1. ....
   ....
2. ....
   ....
3. ....
   ....

Daily Affirmation: I am grateful for this perfect universe that brings me all that I desire.

If we are to teach real peace in this world, and if we are to carry on a real war against war, we shall have to begin with the children.
Mohandas Gandhi

TODAY I AM GRATEFUL FOR: DATE:

1. ....

2. ....

3. ....

....

Daily Affirmation: *I live an independent life that I choose to design however I want.*

TODAY I AM GRATEFUL FOR: DATE:

1. ....

2. ....

3. ....

....

Daily Affirmation: *I am grateful for this perfect universe that brings me all that I desire.*

In prayer it is better to have a heart without words than words without a heart.
Mohandas Gandhi

TODAY I AM GRATEFUL FOR: DATE: ....

1. ....

....

2. ....

....

3. ....

....

Daily Affirmation: I allow myself to prosper.

THOUGHTS FOR THE WEEK: DATE: ....

....

....

....

....

....

....

....

....

....

It is astonishing what an effort it seems to be for many people to put their brains definitely and systematically to work.
Thomas A. Edison

TODAY I AM GRATEFUL FOR: DATE: ....

1. ....

   ....

2. ....

   ....

3. ....

   ....

Daily Affirmation: I enjoy a steady flow of positive energy.

TODAY I AM GRATEFUL FOR: DATE: ....

1. ....

   ....

2. ....

   ....

3. ....

   ....

Daily Affirmation: I am special in many unique ways.

Many of life's failures are people who did not realize how close they were to success when they gave up.
Thomas A. Edison

TODAY I AM GRATEFUL FOR: DATE:

1.

2.

3.

Daily Affirmation: *I prosper wherever I turn and I know that I deserve prosperity of all kinds.*

TODAY I AM GRATEFUL FOR: DATE:

1.

2.

3.

Daily Affirmation: *The more grateful I am, the more reasons I find to be grateful.*

Many of life's failures are people who did not realize how close they were to success when they gave up.
Thomas A. Edison

TODAY I AM GRATEFUL FOR: DATE:

1.

2.

3.

Daily Affirmation: *I prosper wherever I turn and I know that I deserve prosperity of all kinds.*

TODAY I AM GRATEFUL FOR: DATE:

1.

2.

3.

Daily Affirmation: *The more grateful I am, the more reasons I find to be grateful.*

For changes to be of any true value, they've got to be lasting and consistent.
Tony Robbins

TODAY I AM GRATEFUL FOR: DATE:

1.

2.

3.

Daily Affirmation: *This is a rich universe and there is plenty for all of us.*

THOUGHTS FOR THE WEEK: DATE:

Discontent is the first necessity of progress.
Thomas A. Edison

TODAY I AM GRATEFUL FOR: DATE:

1.

2.

3.

Daily Affirmation: I am always supplied with whatever I need.

TODAY I AM GRATEFUL FOR: DATE:

1.

2.

3.

Daily Affirmation: I look for and receive a bountiful supply.

Develop an attitude of gratitude, and give thanks for everything that happens to you, knowing that every step forward is a step toward achieving something bigger and better than your current situation.
Brian Tracy

TODAY I AM GRATEFUL FOR: DATE: ....

1. ....
....
2. ....
....
3. ....
....
....

Daily Affirmation: *My work is always recognized positively.*

TODAY I AM GRATEFUL FOR: DATE: ....

1. ....
....
2. ....
....
3. ....
....
....

Daily Affirmation: I respect my abilities and always work to my full potential.

Develop an attitude of gratitude, and give thanks for everything that happens to you, knowing that every step forward is a step toward achieving something bigger and better than your current situation.
Brian Tracy

TODAY I AM GRATEFUL FOR:　　　DATE: ....

1. ....

2. ....

3. ....

....

Daily Affirmation:　My work is always recognized positively.

TODAY I AM GRATEFUL FOR:　　　DATE: ....

1. ....

2. ....

3. ....

....

Daily Affirmation: I respect my abilities and always work to my full potential.

*Be faithful in small things because it is in them that
your strength lies.
Mother Teresa*

TODAY I AM GRATEFUL FOR: DATE:

1.

2.

3.

*Daily Affirmation: I am in full control of my thoughts
and emotions.*

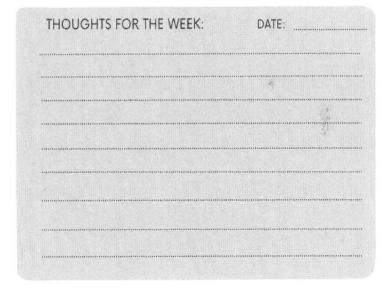

THOUGHTS FOR THE WEEK: DATE:

*Every adversity, every failure, and every heartache, carries
with it the seed of an equivalent or greater benefit.
Napolean Hill*

TODAY I AM GRATEFUL FOR: DATE:

1.

2.

3.

Daily Affirmation: *I accept myself with complete
love and appreciation.*

TODAY I AM GRATEFUL FOR: DATE:

1.

2.

3.

Daily Affirmation: *I feel confident and assured of myself and
my purpose.*

*If you listen to your fears, you will die never knowing what
a great person you might have been.*
Robert H. Schuller

TODODAY I AM GRATEFUL FOR: DATE:

1.

2.

3.

Daily Affirmation: I am a channel of peace and well-being.

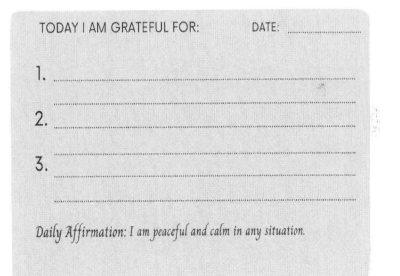

TODAY I AM GRATEFUL FOR: DATE:

1.

2.

3.

Daily Affirmation: I am peaceful and calm in any situation.

If you listen to your fears, you will die never knowing what
a great person you might have been.
Robert H. Schuller

TODAY I AM GRATEFUL FOR: DATE:

1.

2.

3.

Daily Affirmation: *I am a channel of peace and well-being.*

TODAY I AM GRATEFUL FOR: DATE:

1.

2.

3.

Daily Affirmation: I am peaceful and calm in any situation.

Health is the greatest gift, contentment the greatest wealth, faithfulness the best relationship.
Buddha

TODAY I AM GRATEFUL FOR: DATE: ....

1. ....

2. ....

3. ....

Daily Affirmation: *I am filled and surrounded with the positive energy of peace, calm, and well being.*

THOUGHTS FOR THE WEEK: DATE: ....

To keep the body in good health is a duty... otherwise we shall not be able to keep our mind strong and clear.
Buddha

TODAY I AM GRATEFUL FOR: DATE:

1.

2.

3.

Daily Affirmation: *I give and receive the positive energy of peace and love gracefully and easily.*

TODAY I AM GRATEFUL FOR: DATE:

1.

2.

3.

Daily Affirmation: People naturally feel at peace around me.

Attention to health is life greatest hindrance.
Plato

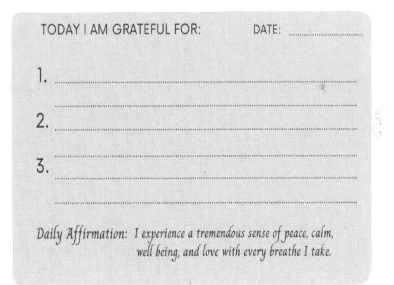

TODAY I AM GRATEFUL FOR: DATE:

1.

2.

3.

Daily Affirmation: *Peaceful energy is always radiating*
within and around me.

TODAY I AM GRATEFUL FOR: DATE:

1.

2.

3.

Daily Affirmation: *I experience a tremendous sense of peace, calm,*
well being, and love with every breathe I take.

Attention to health is life greatest hindrance.
Plato

TODAY I AM GRATEFUL FOR: DATE: ....

1. ....

2. ....

3. ....

Daily Affirmation: *Peaceful energy is always radiating*
within and around me.

TODAY I AM GRATEFUL FOR: DATE: ....

1. ....

2. ....

3. ....

Daily Affirmation: *I experience a tremendous sense of peace, calm,*
well being, and love with every breathe I take.

Health is the greatest possession. Contentment is the greatest treasure. Confidence is the greatest friend. Non-being is the greatest joy.
Lao Tzu

TODAY I AM GRATEFUL FOR: DATE:

1.

2.

3.

Daily Affirmation: *My need for peace within myself is abundantly met.*

THOUGHTS FOR THE WEEK: DATE:

The first wealth is health.
Ralph Waldo Emerson

TODAY I AM GRATEFUL FOR: DATE: ....

1. ....
....

2. ....
....

3. ....
....
....

Daily Affirmation: *The peaceful energy within me radiates*
out and around
the world wherever it is needed.

TODAY I AM GRATEFUL FOR: DATE: ....

1. ....
....

2. ....
....

3. ....
....
....

Daily Affirmation: *I recognize and encourage the*
peaceful nature of others.

The health of the eye seems to demand a horizon. We are never tired, so long as we can see far enough.
Ralph Waldo Emerson

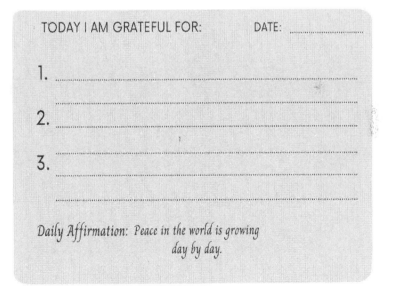

TODAY I AM GRATEFUL FOR: DATE:

1.

2.

3.

Daily Affirmation: *I see a peaceful resolution wherever conflict exists in the world.*

TODAY I AM GRATEFUL FOR: DATE:

1.

2.

3.

Daily Affirmation: *Peace in the world is growing day by day.*

The health of the eye seems to demand a horizon. We are never tired, so long as we can see far enough.
Ralph Waldo Emerson

TODAY I AM GRATEFUL FOR: DATE: ....

1. ....

2. ....

3. ....

....

Daily Affirmation: I see a peaceful resolution wherever conflict exists in the world.

TODAY I AM GRATEFUL FOR: DATE: ....

1. ....

2. ....

3. ....

....

Daily Affirmation: Peace in the world is growing day by day.

What is called genius is the abundance of life and health.
Henry David Thoreau

TODAY I AM GRATEFUL FOR: DATE:

1.

2.

3.

Daily Affirmation: *The positive energy of peace is*
expanding within and
around the people of the world..

THOUGHTS FOR THE WEEK: DATE:

Learning is the beginning of wealth. Learning is the beginning of health. Learning is the beginning of spirituality. Searching and learning is where the miracle process all begins.
Jim Rohn

TODAY I AM GRATEFUL FOR: DATE:

1.

2.

3.

Daily Affirmation: I bring peace into moments of chaos.

TODAY I AM GRATEFUL FOR: DATE:

1.

2.

3.

Daily Affirmation: I attain inner peace by intending my future, and never expecting it.

All mankind... being all equal and independent, no one ought to harm another in his life, health, liberty or possessions.
John Locke

TODAY I AM GRATEFUL FOR: DATE: ....

1. ....

....

2. ....

....

3. ....

....

Daily Affirmation: My life is for living, not
                              for worry or doubt.

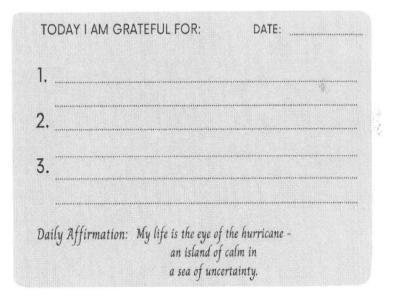

TODAY I AM GRATEFUL FOR: DATE: ....

1. ....

....

2. ....

....

3. ....

....

Daily Affirmation: My life is the eye of the hurricane –
                              an island of calm in
                              a sea of uncertainty.

*All mankind... being all equal and independent, no one ought
to harm another in his life, health, liberty or possessions.*
John Locke

TODAY I AM GRATEFUL FOR: DATE:

1.

2.

3.

Daily Affirmation: *My life is for living, not
for worry or doubt.*

TODAY I AM GRATEFUL FOR: DATE:

1.

2.

3.

Daily Affirmation: *My life is the eye of the hurricane -
an island of calm in
a sea of uncertainty.*

Use your health, even to the point of wearing it out. That is what it is for. Spend all you have before you die; do not outlive yourself.
George Bernard Shaw

TODAY I AM GRATEFUL FOR: DATE:

1.

2.

3.

Daily Affirmation: *Slowly and deeply, I inhale a calming breath.*

THOUGHTS FOR THE WEEK: DATE:

What some call health, if purchased by perpetual anxiety
about diet, isn't much better than tedious disease.
Alexander Pope

TODAY I AM GRATEFUL FOR: DATE: ....

1. ....
   ....
2. ....
   ....
3. ....
   ....
   ....

Daily Affirmation: *Today I embrace simplicity,*
                              peace and solace.

TODAY I AM GRATEFUL FOR: DATE: ....

1. ....
   ....
2. ....
   ....
3. ....
   ....
   ....

Daily Affirmation: *A peaceful heart makes for a*
                              peaceful life.

Health consists with temperance alone.
Alexander Pope

TODAY I AM GRATEFUL FOR: DATE: ....

1. ....

....

2. ....

....

3. ....

....

....

Daily Affirmation: *I trust the universe to deliver my*
highest good in every situation.

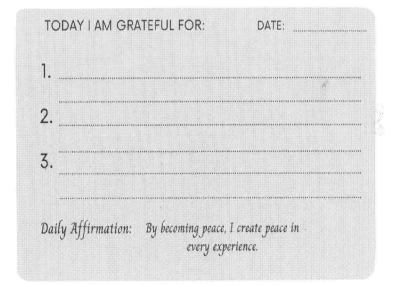

TODAY I AM GRATEFUL FOR: DATE: ....

1. ....

....

2. ....

....

3. ....

....

....

Daily Affirmation: *By becoming peace, I create peace in*
every experience.

Health consists with temperance alone.
Alexander Pope

TODAY I AM GRATEFUL FOR: DATE:

1.

2.

3.

Daily Affirmation: I trust the universe to deliver my
                     highest good in every situation.

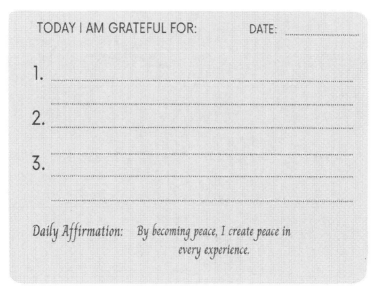

TODAY I AM GRATEFUL FOR: DATE:

1.

2.

3.

Daily Affirmation: By becoming peace, I create peace in
                     every experience.

Happiness is nothing more than good health and a bad memory.
Albert Schweitzer

TODAY I AM GRATEFUL FOR: DATE:

1.

2.

3.

Daily Affirmation: *I am filled with the light of love, peace and joy.*

THOUGHTS FOR THE WEEK: DATE:

When wealth is lost, nothing is lost; when health is lost,
something is lost; when character is lost, all is lost.
Billy Graham

TODAY I AM GRATEFUL FOR: DATE:

1.

2.

3.

Daily Affirmation: *Today my mission is to*
surrender and release.

TODAY I AM GRATEFUL FOR: DATE:

1.

2.

3.

Daily Affirmation: *I am at peace with my choices in life.*

It's no measure of health to be well adjusted to a profoundly sick society.
Jiddu Krishnamurti

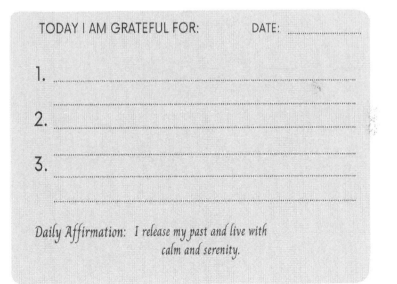

TODAY I AM GRATEFUL FOR: DATE: ....

1. ....

....

2. ....

....

3. ....

....

Daily Affirmation: *I choose a peaceful and calm spirit.*

TODAY I AM GRATEFUL FOR: DATE: ....

1. ....

....

2. ....

....

3. ....

....

Daily Affirmation: *I release my past and live with*
calm and serenity.

It's no measure of health to be well adjusted to a profoundly sick society.
Jiddu Krishnamurti

TODAY I AM GRATEFUL FOR: DATE:

1.

2.

3.

Daily Affirmation: I choose a peaceful and calm spirit.

TODAY I AM GRATEFUL FOR: DATE:

1.

2.

3.

Daily Affirmation: I release my past and live with
                     calm and serenity.

Medicine sometimes snatches away health, sometimes
gives it.
Ovid

TODAY I AM GRATEFUL FOR: DATE: ....

1. ....
....

2. ....
....

3. ....
....

Daily Affirmation: *I am free to be me and express*
                      myself openly.

THOUGHTS FOR THE WEEK: DATE: ....

The wish for healing has always been half of health.
Lucius Annaeus Seneca

TODAY I AM GRATEFUL FOR: DATE: ....

1. ....

....

2. ....

....

3. ....

....

....

Daily Affirmation: *I am aware of all of the*
beauty around me.

TODAY I AM GRATEFUL FOR: DATE: ....

1. ....

....

2. ....

....

3. ....

....

....

Daily Affirmation: *I embrace my oneness with nature, the seasons, the*
sky, and all of the colors, smells and textures.

Health is the state about which medicine has nothing to say.
W. H. Auden

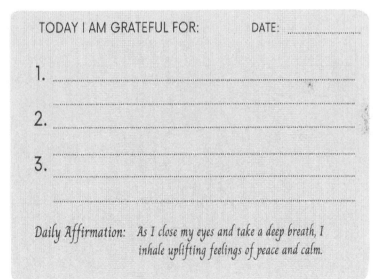

TODO I AM GRATEFUL FOR: DATE: ....

1. ....
....
2. ....
....
3. ....
....

Daily Affirmation: *I take time for spiritual connection*
in meditation or prayer.

TODAY I AM GRATEFUL FOR: DATE: ....

1. ....
....
2. ....
....
3. ....
....

Daily Affirmation: *As I close my eyes and take a deep breath, I*
inhale uplifting feelings of peace and calm.

Health is the state about which medicine has nothing to say.
W. H. Auden

TODAY I AM GRATEFUL FOR: DATE:

1.

2.

3.

Daily Affirmation: *I take time for spiritual connection*
in meditation or prayer.

TODAY I AM GRATEFUL FOR: DATE:

1.

2.

3.

Daily Affirmation: *As I close my eyes and take a deep breath, I*
inhale uplifting feelings of peace and calm.

It's bizarre that the produce manager is more important
to my children's health than the pediatrician.
Meryl Streep

TODAY I AM GRATEFUL FOR: DATE: ....

1. ....

2. ....

3. ....

....

Daily Affirmation: I exhale and release any tension
or stress.

THOUGHTS FOR THE WEEK: DATE: ....

....

....

....

....

....

....

....

....

The greatest of follies is to sacrifice health for any other kind of happiness.
Arthur Schopenhauer

TODAY I AM GRATEFUL FOR: DATE:

1.

2.

3.

Daily Affirmation: I deserve to relax.

TODAY I AM GRATEFUL FOR: DATE:

1.

2.

3.

Daily Affirmation: As I stop and relax, I refresh my mind, my body and my spirit.

In a disordered mind, as in a disordered body, soundness of health is impossible.
Marcus Tullius Cicero

TODAY I AM GRATEFUL FOR: DATE:

1.

2.

3.

Daily Affirmation: *No matter what events occur during my day I remain calm and centered.*

TODAY I AM GRATEFUL FOR: DATE:

1.

2.

3.

Daily Affirmation: *I let go of worry.*

In a disordered mind, as in a disordered body, soundness of health is impossible.
Marcus Tullius Cicero

TODAY I AM GRATEFUL FOR: DATE: ....

1. ....

2. ....

3. ....

....

Daily Affirmation: *No matter what events occur during my day I remain calm and centered.*

TODAY I AM GRATEFUL FOR: DATE: ....

1. ....

2. ....

3. ....

....

Daily Affirmation: *I let go of worry.*

He who has health, has hope; and he who has hope, has
everything.
Thomas Carlyle

TODAY I AM GRATEFUL FOR: DATE: ....

1. ....
   ....
2. ....
   ....
3. ....
   ....

Daily Affirmation: *I enjoy the natural flow of this*
                       day; whatever it may bring.

THOUGHTS FOR THE WEEK: DATE: ....

....
....
....
....
....
....
....
....

Time and health are two precious assets that we don't recognize and appreciate until they have been depleted.
Denis Waitley

TODAY I AM GRATEFUL FOR: DATE:

1.

2.

3.

Daily Affirmation: I offer myself a day of nurturing this week.

TODAY I AM GRATEFUL FOR: DATE:

1.

2.

3.

Daily Affirmation: I live and enjoy fully the present moment.

*If we could give every individual the right amount of
nourishment and exercise, not too little and not too much,
we would have found the safest way to health.*
Hippocrates

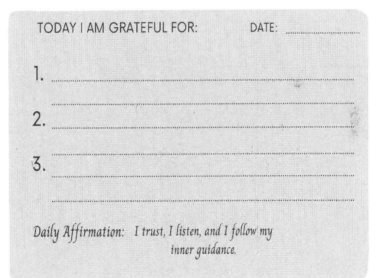

TODAY I AM GRATEFUL FOR: DATE:

1.

2.

3.

Daily Affirmation: I open my heart to receiving love
fully today.

TODAY I AM GRATEFUL FOR: DATE:

1.

2.

3.

Daily Affirmation: I trust, I listen, and I follow my
inner guidance.

If we could give every individual the right amount of
nourishment and exercise, not too little and not too much,
we would have found the safest way to health.
Hippocrates

TODAY I AM GRATEFUL FOR: DATE:

1.

2.

3.

Daily Affirmation: I open my heart to receiving love
fully today.

TODAY I AM GRATEFUL FOR: DATE:

1.

2.

3.

Daily Affirmation: I trust, I listen, and I follow my
inner guidance.

A wise man should consider that health is the greatest of
human blessings, and learn how by his own thought to
derive benefit from his illnesses.
Hippocrates

TODAY I AM GRATEFUL FOR: DATE: ....

1. ....

   ....

2. ....

   ....

3. ....

   ....

Daily Affirmation: *All my relationships are loving*
                     and harmonious.

THOUGHTS FOR THE WEEK: DATE: ....

....

....

....

....

....

....

....

....

*Treasure the love you receive above all. It will survive long
after your good health has vanished.
Og Mandino*

TODAY I AM GRATEFUL FOR: DATE:

1.

2.

3.

Daily Affirmation: I am at one with the inner child in me.

TODAY I AM GRATEFUL FOR: DATE:

1.

2.

3.

Daily Affirmation: I trust in the process of life.

Medicine to produce health must examine disease; and music, to create harmony must investigate discord.
Plutarch

TODAY I AM GRATEFUL FOR: DATE:

1.

2.

3.

Daily Affirmation: I love life and life loves me.

TODAY I AM GRATEFUL FOR: DATE:

1.

2.

3.

Daily Affirmation: I am a beautiful being of light.

Medicine to produce health must examine disease; and music, to create harmony must investigate discord.
Plutarch

TODAY I AM GRATEFUL FOR: DATE:

1.

2.

3.

Daily Affirmation: I love life and life loves me.

TODAY I AM GRATEFUL FOR: DATE:

1.

2.

3.

Daily Affirmation: I am a beautiful being of light.

A woman's health is her capital.
Harriet Beecher Stowe

TODAY I AM GRATEFUL FOR: DATE: ....

1. ....

2. ....

3. ....

....

Daily Affirmation: I look upon God, and the Divine within
to be the source my happiness.

THOUGHTS FOR THE WEEK: DATE: ....

....
....
....
....
....
....
....
....

We know a great deal more about the causes of physical disease than we do about the causes of physical health.
M. Scott Peck

TODAY I AM GRATEFUL FOR: DATE: ....

1. ....

....

2. ....

....

3. ....

....

Daily Affirmation: *I am beautiful both on the inside*
and outside.

TODAY I AM GRATEFUL FOR: DATE: ....

1. ....

....

2. ....

....

3. ....

....

Daily Affirmation: *I am acting from my higher self.*

A kiss makes the heart young again and wipes out the years.
Rupert Brooke

TODAY I AM GRATEFUL FOR: DATE: ....

1. ....

2. ....

3. ....

....

Daily Affirmation: I honor who I am.

TODAY I AM GRATEFUL FOR: DATE: ....

1. ....

2. ....

3. ....

....

Daily Affirmation: I see the world through eyes of
love and acceptance.

*We know a great deal more about the causes of physical
disease than we do about the causes of physical health.*
M. Scott Peck

TODAY I AM GRATEFUL FOR: DATE: ....

1. ....
   ....
2. ....
   ....
3. ....
   ....

Daily Affirmation: I am beautiful both on the inside
and outside.

TODAY I AM GRATEFUL FOR: DATE: ....

1. ....
   ....
2. ....
   ....
3. ....
   ....

Daily Affirmation: I am acting from my higher self.

A loving heart is the beginning of all knowledge.
Thomas Carlyle

TODAY I AM GRATEFUL FOR: DATE:

1.

2.

3.

Daily Affirmation: *I willingly release any need for*
struggle or suffering.

THOUGHTS FOR THE WEEK: DATE:

Come live in my heart, and pay no rent.
Samuel Lover

TODAY I AM GRATEFUL FOR: DATE: ....

1. ....

....

2. ....

....

3. ....

....

Daily Affirmation: *I love myself exactly as I am.*

TODAY I AM GRATEFUL FOR: DATE: ....

1. ....

....

2. ....

....

3. ....

....

Daily Affirmation: *I no longer wait to be perfect in*
order to love myself.

Do all things with love.
Og Mandino

TODAY I AM GRATEFUL FOR: DATE:

1.

2.

3.

Daily Affirmation: *I am a creature unlike any other - truly*
unique and blessed.

TODAY I AM GRATEFUL FOR: DATE:

1.

2.

3.

Daily Affirmation: *I move through life knowing that I am*
divinely protected and guided.

Do all things with love.
Og Mandino

TODAY I AM GRATEFUL FOR: DATE: ....

1. ....
....

2. ....
....

3. ....
....

Daily Affirmation: *I am a creature unlike any other - truly*
unique and blessed.

TODAY I AM GRATEFUL FOR: DATE: ....

1. ....
....

2. ....
....

3. ....
....

Daily Affirmation: *I move through life knowing that I am*
divinely protected and guided.

First love is only a little foolishness and a lot of curiosity.
George Bernard Shaw

TODAY I AM GRATEFUL FOR: DATE: ....

1. ....

2. ....

3. ....

....

Daily Affirmation: *I can do all things through Spirit who strengthens me.*

THOUGHTS FOR THE WEEK: DATE: ....

Fortune and love favor the brave.
Ovid

TODAY I AM GRATEFUL FOR: DATE:

1.

2.

3.

Daily Affirmation: It's a fabulous day for singing a song.

TODAY I AM GRATEFUL FOR: DATE:

1.

2.

3.

Daily Affirmation: I attract miracles into my life now.

Fortune and love favor the brave.
Ovid

TODAY I AM GRATEFUL FOR: DATE: ....

1. ....

2. ....

3. ....

....

Daily Affirmation: *It's a fabulous day for singing a song.*

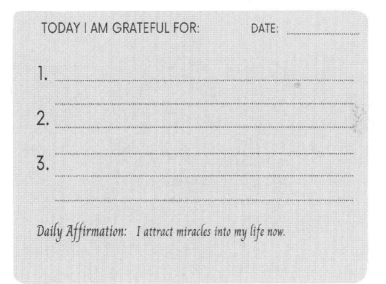

TODAY I AM GRATEFUL FOR: DATE: ....

1. ....

2. ....

3. ....

....

Daily Affirmation: *I attract miracles into my life now.*

I have found the paradox, that if you love until it hurts,
there can be no more hurt, only more love.
Daphne Rae

TODAY I AM GRATEFUL FOR: DATE:

1.

2.

3.

Daily Affirmation: I deeply and truly love and
approve of myself.

TODAY I AM GRATEFUL FOR: DATE:

1.

2.

3.

Daily Affirmation: I love who I am.

If you could only love enough, you could be the most powerful person in the world.
Emmet Fox

TODAY I AM GRATEFUL FOR: DATE: ....

1. ....

....

2. ....

....

3. ....

....

Daily Affirmation: I trust in love.

THOUGHTS FOR THE WEEK: DATE: ....

....
....
....
....
....
....
....
....